Comets

by
Melanie Chrismer

Children's Press®
A Division of Scholastic Inc.
New York Toronto London Auckland Sydney
Mexico City New Delhi Hong Kong
Danbury, Connecticut

These content vocabulary word builders
are for grades 1-2.

Consultant: Daniel D. Kelson, Ph.D.
Carnegie Observatories
Pasadena, CA

Reading Specialist: Don Curry

Photo Credits:

Photographs © 2005: Corbis Images/Ali Jarekji/Reuters: 17; Digital Vision: 5 bottom left, 15; Getty Images/Francesco Reginato/The Image Bank: 4 bottom left, 9; Photo Researchers, NY: 5 top right (Chris Butler), 4 top, 20 bottom, 21, 23 (John Chumack), 4 bottom right, 13 (Claus Lunau/FOCI/Bonnier Pub.), 11 (Pekka Parviainen), 2, 5 bottom right, 20 top, 23 spot art (Kitt Peak/Aura), 19 (Rev. Ronald Royer), cover, 1, 5 top left, 7 (Frank Zullo); PhotoDisc/Getty Images via SODA: back cover.

Book Design: Simonsays Design!

Library of Congress Cataloging-in-Publication Data

Chrismer, Melanie.
    Comets / by Melanie Chrismer.
        p. cm. — (Scholastic news nonfiction readers)
    Includes bibliographical references and index.
    ISBN 0-516-24949-5 (lib. bdg.)
    1. Comets—Juvenile literature. I. Title. II. Series.
    QB721.5.C57 2005
    523.6—dc22
                                2005002836

1 2 3 4 5 6 7 8 9 10 R 14 13 12 11 10 09 08 07 06 05

CONTENTS

WORD HUNT

Look for these words as you read. They will be in **bold**.

coma
(**koh**-muh)

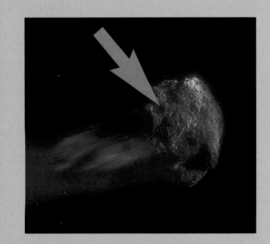

nucleus
(**noo**-klee-uhss)

Oort Cloud
(ort kloud)

4

comet
(**kom**-it)

Kuiper Belt
(**keye**-per belt)

orbit
(**or**-bit)

outer space
(**ou**-tur spayss)

5

Comets!

Can you catch a **comet** by one of its tails?

No. One tail is made of dust. The other tail is made of gas.

There is nothing to hold onto.

dust

gas

A comet is a big ball
of frozen water, gases,
and dust.

When a comet gets close
to the Sun, it changes.

The Sun heats up the comet.

The center, or **nucleus,** of
the comet stays frozen.

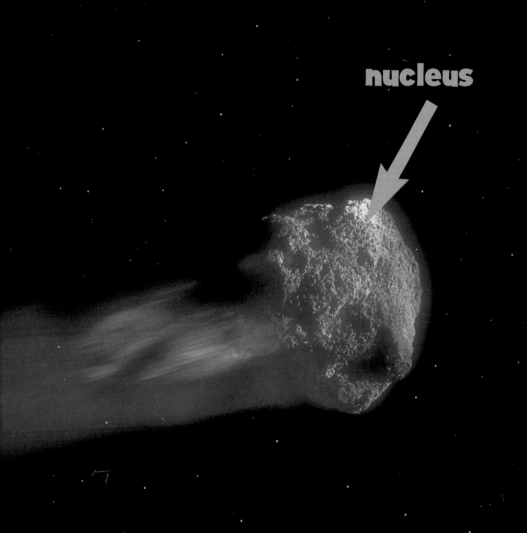

nucleus

The surface of the comet starts to melt.

This makes a cloud around the nucleus called a **coma**.

Two tails are formed.

One tail is dust coming off the comet.

The other tail is made of gas.

This comet is heating up.

dust tail

gas tail

Scientists think comets come from the **Kuiper Belt** or the **Oort Cloud**.

The Kuiper Belt is near Neptune.

The Oort Cloud is very far out in space.

This painting shows comets leaving the Oort Cloud.

Some comets **orbit** the Sun.

We do not see them all the time, like we can see planets.

Comets orbit very far away in **outer space**.

Some do not come back for a long time.

Sun

comet

This comet is orbiting the Sun.

Some comets leave pieces behind.

The comet Swift-Tuttle left a path of dust and rock.

Every August, Earth passes through the path of comet pieces.

The pieces of the comet are called shooting stars!

A special camera took this picture of shooting stars one night in August.

You can see shooting stars in August.

First, find a place away from city lights.

Stay awake and keep your eyes on the sky.

Then, make a wish on a shooting star!

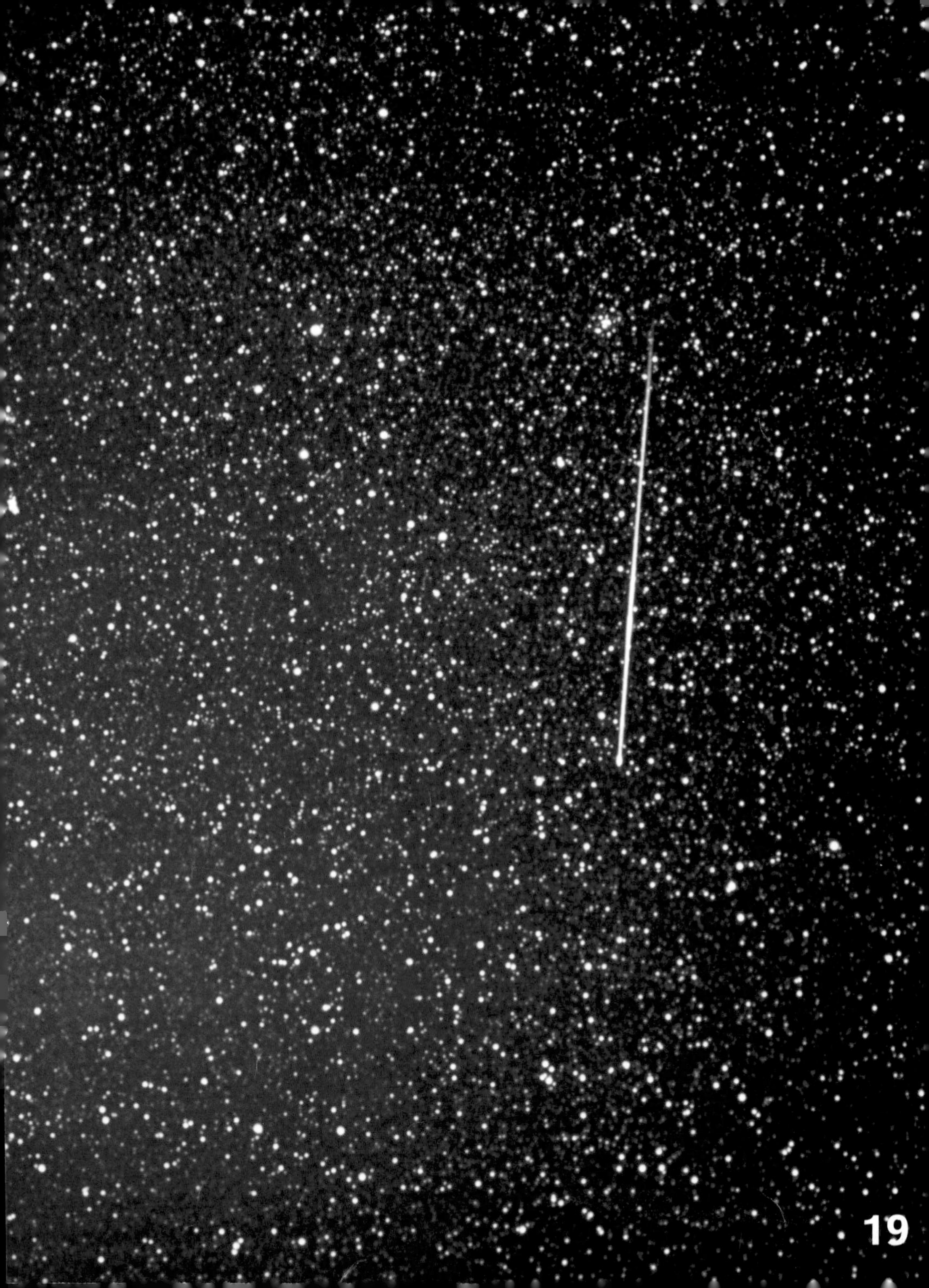

Famous Comets!

What is the most famous comet? Halley's comet!
It was discovered in 1705.
We won't see it again until the year 2061.

Did you see comet Neat?
It was here in May 2004.

Look! It's comet Hale-Bopp.
Look at it glow.
It was discovered in 1995.

This is comet Hyakutake.
Scientists know that comet Hyakutake
orbitted the Sun in 15,500 B.C.

YOUR NEW WORDS

coma (**koh**-muh) a glowing cloud of gas and dust around a comet

comet (**kom**-it) a big dusty ball of ice that travels around the Sun in a long slow path

Kuiper Belt (**keye**-per belt) an area past Neptune where many icy objects orbit the Sun

nucleus (**noo**-klee-uhss) the center of a comet

Oort Cloud (ort kloud) an area past Pluto where there are many comets

orbit (**or**-bit) the path around an object

outer space (**ou**-tur spayss) everything past the planet Earth and its atmosphere

Comets Are Amazing!

The word "comet" comes from the Greek word *kometes*. This means "very long hair".

When a comet heats up, part of it stays frozen and part does not.

A comet's tail can be a million miles long.

Comets are big dusty balls of ice.

Comets have four parts: a nucleus, a coma, and two tails.

FIND OUT MORE

Book:
Killer Rocks from Outer Space: Asteroids, Comets, and Meteors
Steven N. Koppes, Lerner Publications Group, 2004

Website:
Comet Information and Pictures
http://stardust.jpl.nasa.gov/classroom/cometkids.html
http://starchild.gsfc.nasa.gov/docs/StarChild/solar_system_level1/comets.html

MEET THE AUTHOR:

Melanie Chrismer grew up near NASA in Houston, Texas. She loves math and science and has written 12 books for children. To write her books, she visited NASA where she floated in the zero-gravity trainer called the Vomit Comet. She says, "it is the best roller coaster ever!"